Tyler Fuller is an adoptive father, pastor, TBRI® Practitioner, and freelance writer based in the Florida panhandle. All words and illustrations by Tyler Fuller.

More About The Pearl Project: **ThePearlProject.org**

Some concepts in this resource are informed or derived from an intervention called Trust Based Relational Intervention® (TBRI®), developed by TCU's Karyn Purvis Institute for Child Development (KPICD).
For more information about TBRI® visit **Child.tcu.edu.**

For permission requests or further information contact the author: Tyler@thepearlproject.org

WELCOME!

ATTACHMENT

THE BOND BETWEEN YOU AND YOUR CAREGIVERS IS CALLED ATTACHMENT! THE WAY WE RELATE TO THE PEOPLE WE LOVE WILL BE PART OF HOW WE LOVE OTHERS WHEN WE GROW UP!

Understanding our own "attachment style" can help us become better at building secure relationships with the people we love. The Karyn Purvis Institute of Child Development has an excellent 3 minute video that describes the process and styles. Search the internet for "TBRI Animate- attachment."

B BRAIN

YOUR BRAIN IS AMAZING!
YOUR "DOWNSTAIRS BRAIN" HELPS RUN ALL OF THE SYSTEMS THAT KEEP YOUR BODY WORKING AND SAFE. YOUR "UPSTAIRS BRAIN" HAS THE POWER TO CREATE, EXPLORE, PLAN, BUILD, ENGINEER, AND CONNECT WITH OTHER PEOPLE.

Every one of us has an "upstairs brain" that is great at planning for the future, self-reflection, focus, building relationships, and all sorts of complex thought. We all also have a "downstairs brain" (or "survival brain") that is an expert at keeping us safe. One way the "downstairs brain" keeps us safe is by taking control of our body and mind and making fast decisions when it senses danger. Dan Siegel's "hand model of the brain" is a simple way to understand this dynamic.

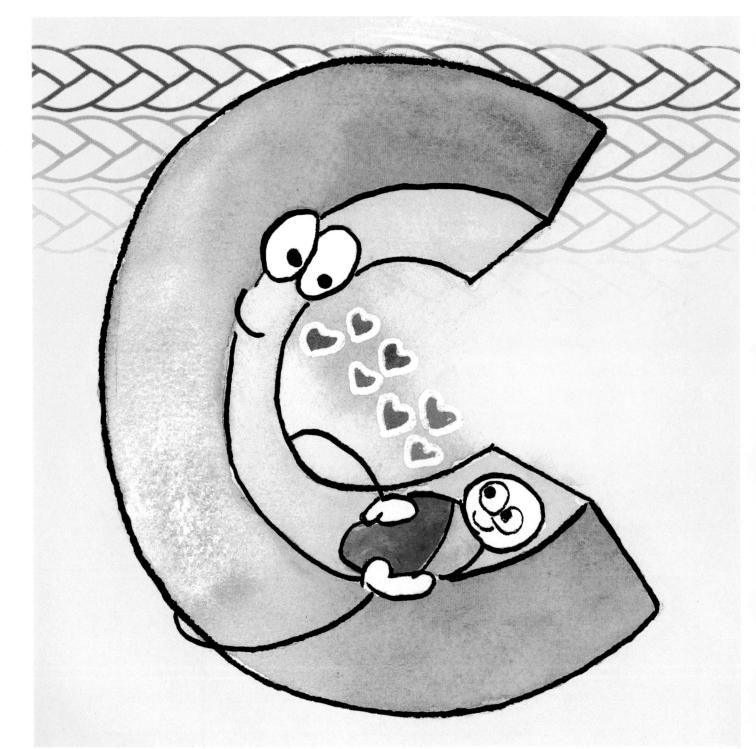

CONNECTION

WHEN WE HAVE NEEDS, WE NEED TO LET SOMEONE KNOW. THIS IS WHY BABIES CRY WHEN THEY NEED MILK.
WHEN A LOVING CAREGIVER MEETS THOSE NEEDS, WE START THE BEAUTIFUL AND POWERFUL PROCESS OF CONNECTION!

Connection is built when caregivers continually identify and meet the needs of the kids they care for. When caregivers see and meet needs, we aren't only building connection with that child, we are teaching them <u>how</u> to connect with others throughout their lifetime. The cycle of expressing needs and having them met teaches our child that they have a voice in the world and that their needs matter. Connection is the cornerstone of trauma-informed care.

D DANCE !

LET'S TAKE A QUICK BREAK FROM READING AND DO A "MIRROR DANCE!" IF YOU'RE READING WITH A FRIEND, SIMPLY TAKE TURNS SHOWING OFF A COOL DANCE MOVE WHILE YOUR FRIEND COPIES YOUR MOVES! IF YOU'RE READING ALONE, DANCE IN FRONT OF A MIRROR. BE YOUR OWN PARTNER!

Play builds connection, and dancing helps move us from blue to green (see the emotions thermometer page at the end of the book). The "Mirror Dance" activity is a playful way to show our kids that they are seen and valued - we demonstrate that they have voice, and that we are listening by seeing their moves and then doing them ourselves. You can show some of your moves as well, and watch your kids respond!

E EMOTIONS

SOMETIMES EMOTIONS CAN BE BIG, BOLD, AND BRIGHT
* JOY * ANGER * LOVE * FEAR *
THEY CAN ALSO BE SMALL AND QUIET
>FRUSTRATION< >JEALOUSLY< >PRIDE<
BUT THERE ARE NO BAD EMOTIONS. EMOTIONS TELL US
SOMETHING ABOUT WHAT IS GOING ON IN OUR HEARTS
AND MINDS.

Understanding and validating the emotional experiences of our kids is an important way to help them feel seen and heard. Recognizing and naming feelings is a powerful tool for both caregivers and kids. Putting a "Feelings Chart" in your home is a great way to help kids name their feelings!

F

FIGHT, FLIGHT, FREEZE !

WHEN THE "DOWNSTAIRS BRAIN" SENSES DANGER, IT SENDS SIGNALS ALL OVER YOUR BODY THAT SAY:

"GET TO SAFETY NOW!"

IF YOU WERE IN THE WOODS, AND SAW A BEAR - YOUR BODY MAY AUTOMATICALLY TELL YOU TO STAND YOUR GROUND (FIGHT), RUN AWAY (FLIGHT), OR IT MAY SHUT DOWN ALTOGETHER, LIKE A TURTLE IN IT'S SHELL (FREEZE)

When fear has triggered a "downstairs brain" response, the "upstairs brain" is totally offline. We can't have reason-filled conversations or talk about future implications with kids until we've demonstrated that we can provide safety and calmly helped turn off all of the alarms in their brains and bodies. The "downstairs brain" alarms are very sensitive in kids who have experienced trauma. "The Guard Dog and The Owl" by Cosmic Kids Yoga is an excellent YouTube video that explains this process for kids.

G GREEN

WHEN WE'RE IN A MOOD THAT IS CONTENT, READY TO MAKE FRIENDS, AND ABLE TO LISTEN AND GROW, WE ARE "IN THE GREEN." SOMETIMES WE FEEL A LITTLE SLOW, OR SAD, OR TIRED, LIKE OUR BODY AND MIND ARE HEAVY, THOSE ARE "BLUE" FEELINGS. SOMETIMES WE ARE FEELING EXCITED, HYPER, MAYBE EVEN ANGRY OR LOUD, THAT'S BEING "IN THE RED." WHEN WE RECOGNIZE WHAT COLOR WE ARE, WE CAN USE TOOLS TO HELP US GET BACK "IN THE GREEN."

The Emotions Thermometer (see the end of this book) is a simple tool that caregivers and parents can use to identify how we're feeling. There is nothing wrong with feeling "blue "or "red," but it is helpful to have some strategies to move into the green, for ourselves or the kids we work with. Physical activity, protein snacks, sour or spicy candy, and energetic music can help us move from "blue" to "green." Deep breathing, physical activity, snacks and water, and calming music can help us move from "red" to "green." "Green" is where growth, learning, and relationship building happen best.

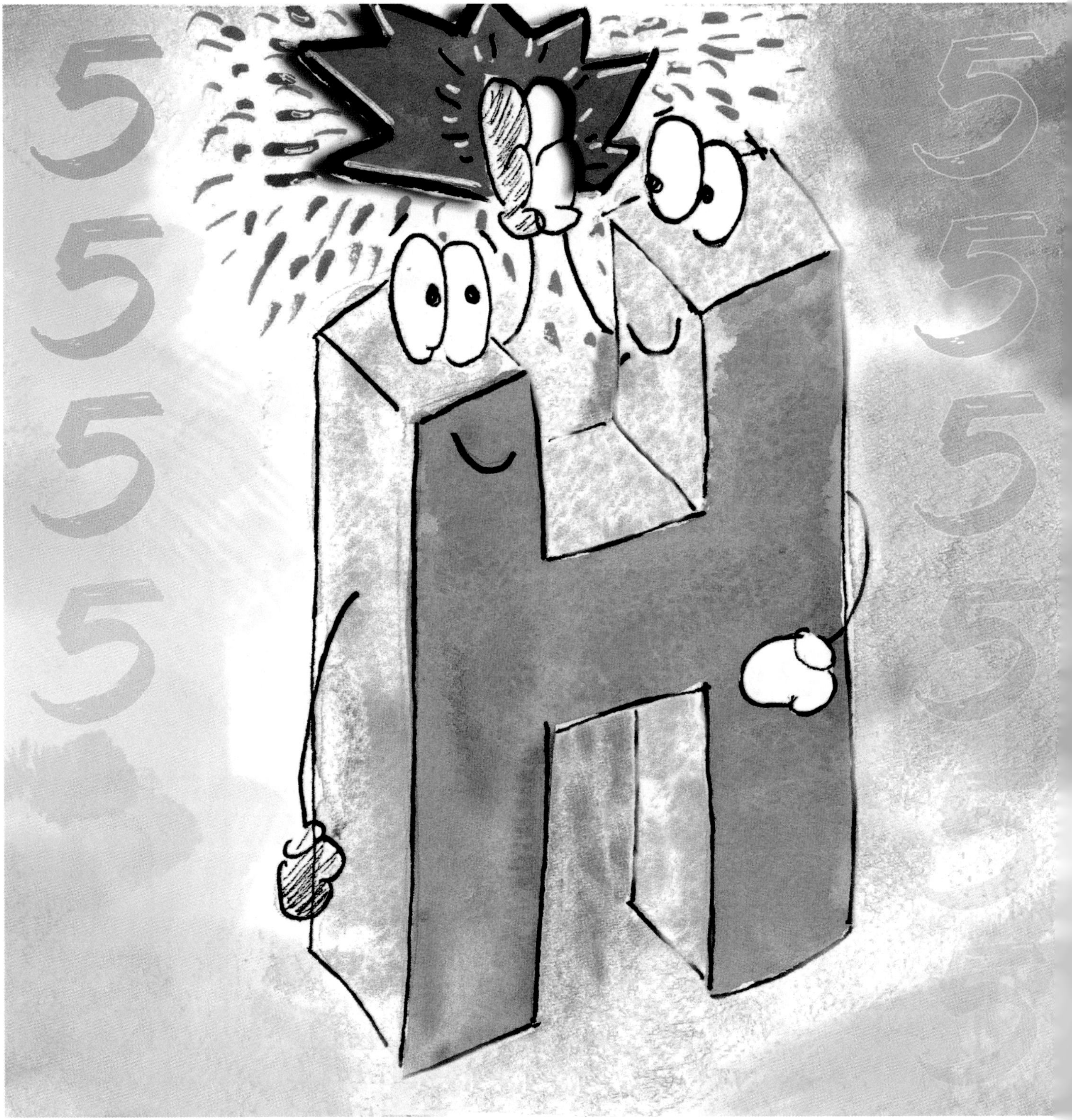
5
5
5
5
5
5
5
5
5

HIGH FIVE

STOP READING – QUICK!!
GIVE EVERYONE IN THE ROOM A HIGH FIVE
GO!

Finding ways that our kids are comfortable with incorporating touch helps us tap into the universal language of caregiving - loving, healthy touch! Are hugs out of bounds, what about high fives? Arm wrestling and thumb wars combine touch and play! If a kid isn't comfortable with any kind of touch you can offer "air high fives" or other creative versions of "virtual touch" to begin to build trust.

I FEEL
I WANT
I NEED
I IMAG
I WOUL
I AM I
I WANT
EED
EEL
T I IMAGINE
I FEEL I
INE I WANT
I AM
I NEED I
KE I LIKE
I AM I
I

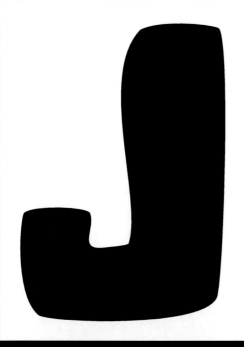

JUMPING JACKS

WE HAVE BEEN READING FOR A FEW MINUTES, MAYBE WE'RE FEELING A LITTLE BLUE, OR SLOOOWW. LET'S GET UP AND DO 10 JUMPING JACKS TOGETHER TO GET BACK IN THAT GREEN ZONE! READY? GO!

Physical activity, especially activities that use a large range of motion and engage a variety of muscle groups, can be an incredibly helpful tool to help our kids get "in the green" if they're feeling sad, or sluggish, or depressed, or lacking motivation. It's true for us as well! Sometimes a quick burst of physical activity can help us get right back where we need to be in order to provide the best care.

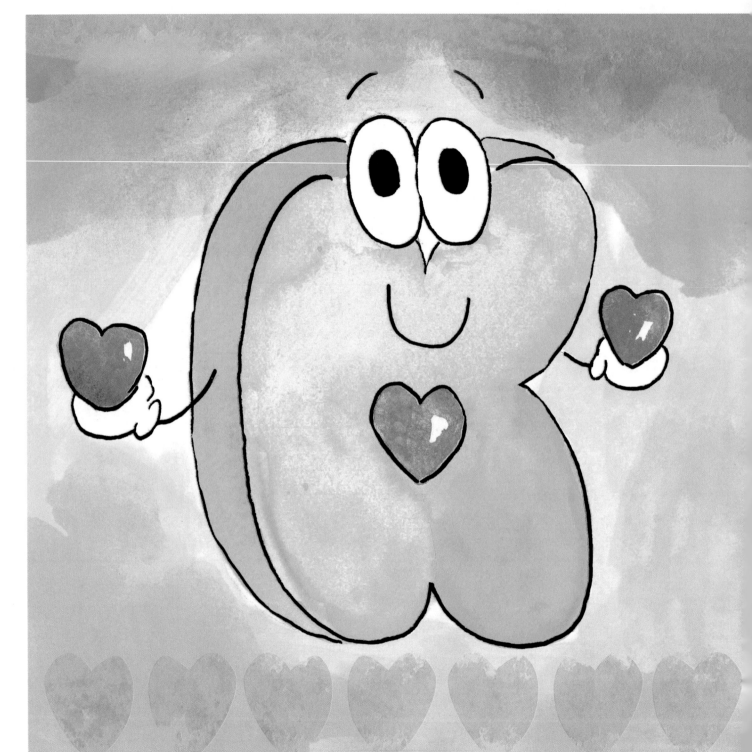

K KINDNESS

WE ALL WANT TO BE TREATED WITH KINDNESS, AND WE CAN ALL BE KIND TO OTHERS. WHEN WE LISTEN WELL, THINK ABOUT HOW OTHERS FEEL, AND ACT WITH GENTLENESS – WE'RE SPREADING KINDNESS! HERE'S A NEAT FACT, WE CAN BE KIND TO OURSELVES TOO!

We can cultivate kindness in the kids we care for when we model good listening and use empathy to try to understand how they feel. The job that we are doing is very, very challenging - it's worth extending some kindness and gentleness towards our view of ourself as a caregivers as well!   Empathy, listening, and kindness are foundational to giving trauma-informed care.

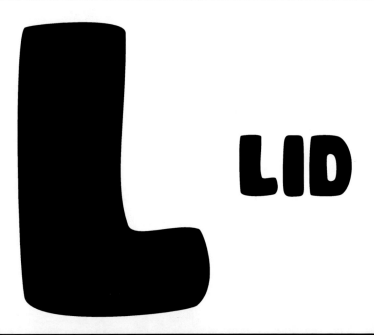

L LID

"FLIPPING OUR LID" IS WHEN OUR EMOTIONS GET REAAAALLLLLY BIG AND TAKE CONTROL OVER OUR BODIES AND MINDS. REMEMBER LETTER "F" AND "B?" WHEN WE FLIP OUR LIDS, THE "DOWNSTAIRS BRAIN" IS IN CONTROL! CAN YOU THINK BACK TO THE LAST TIME THAT YOU FLIPPED YOUR LID? TELL US ABOUT IT!

Caregivers and kids both have lids, and we're both capable of flipping them sometimes! Can you share with the kid you're reading with about the last time you flipped your lid? When the "downstairs brain" is in control, a trauma-informed response starts with getting the lid back on. Nothing good can happen until we're all regulated and "in the green" again. When the lid is flipped - consequences, future planning, and even cause/effect reasoning are all out of reach.

M MINDFULNESS

MINDFULNESS IS ABOUT TURNING OUR EYES AND EARS INWARD, TO LOOK FOR AND LISTEN TO WHAT'S GOING ON INSIDE OF US. MINDFULNESS HELPS US UNDERSTAND WHAT OUR EMOTIONS ARE TELLING US - LET'S TRY IT!
TAKE A DEEP BREATH. CLOSE YOUR EYES. THINK ABOUT WHAT YOU'RE SENSING - WHAT YOU HEAR, SMELL, AND FEEL.
NOW THINK ABOUT WHAT YOU FEEL, RIGHT NOW IN THIS MOMENT.
NOW THAT YOU'VE LOOKED INSIDE TO DISCOVER HOW YOU FEEL, CAN YOU USE A FEW WORDS TO DESCRIBE HOW YOU FEEL?

Knowing how <u>we</u> are feeling and what <u>we</u> are bringing to the table helps us to have more thoughtful interactions with our kids - are we happy, sad, tired or stressed? That's okay (be kind to yourself), but mindfulness helps us recognize that we are bringing those things into the interactions we have with our kids. Mindfulness is a tool that simply helps us stay aware of what's going on in us.

N NEED

WE ALL HAVE NEEDS, SOMETIMES IT'S EASY TO NAME THEM, SOMETIMES IT'S TOUGH. OUR BODY TELLS US WHEN WE NEED THINGS: IF WE NEED FOOD WE GET HUNGRY, IF WE NEED REST WE GET SLEEPY! LEARNING TO IDENTIFY AND EXPRESS WHAT WE NEED HELPS US GET THOSE NEEDS MET.

When we see the kids we love expressing BIG emotions, or flipping their lid over something that seems trivial - the first question we should ask is: <u>what is the need behind this behavior</u>, and how can I help meet that need? It can be as simple as identifying a temper tantrum as a "hangry" moment, or as complex as recognizing situations that seem normal to us but put our kids need for "felt safety" into overdrive! If we aren't sure what the need is, we can try asking our child: "What do you need?"

OVERLOAD

OUR SENSES ARE SO GREAT! WE EXPERIENCE THE WORLD, AND ALL OF IT'S BEAUTY THROUGH OUR SENSES. BUT SOMETIMES THE THINGS OUR SENSES ARE TAKING IN CAN FEEL OVERWHELMING - OVERLOAD! HAVE YOU EVER BEEN IN A REALLY BRIGHT, LOUD, OR STINKY ROOM? HOW DID IT MAKE YOU FEEL? OUR SENSES CAN ALSO HELP CALM US DOWN. NICE SMELLS, QUIET MUSIC, WEIGHTED BLANKETS, AND SOFT CUDDLY TOYS, CAN ALL ENGAGE OUR SENSES TO HELP US RELAX WHEN WE'RE FEELING OVERWHELMED.

Sometimes kids who have experienced trauma can have a chaotic relationship with their senses. Some of our kids are extremely sensitive, sensory inputs that seem small to us can feel huge to them! Some of our kids are the exact opposite, they crave input. Learning what our kids' sensory needs are can help us meet those needs in helpful ways. Sensory input can also be an answer to the question "What's the need behind the behavior?" Check the "Sensory Diet" page at the end of this book for more information.

PPLAY

PLAYING TOGETHER IS A GREAT WAY TO CONNECT.
LET'S PLAY NOW!
TAKE A BREAK FROM READING FOR A QUICK ROUND OF ROCK, PAPER, SCISSORS!

"Play Disarms Fear" -Dr. Karyn Purvis
Play is a great tool for caregivers to use to build connection with kids and to defuse difficult situations. Play teaches kids healthy interactions in a fun way and can do wonders for the overall "vibe" of a caregiving relationship. As caregivers we may not always be in the mood for play, but even 5-10 minutes of play can do wonders for our connection with our kids.

QUICK FIX

SOMETIMES, WHEN WE ARE INTERACTING WITH OUR FRIENDS OR OUR GROWN-UPS, WE MAKE THE WRONG DECISION. WHEN OUR HEART AND BRAIN TELL US "THAT WASN'T THE BEST WAY," WE HAVE A CHANCE TO MAKE IT RIGHT! A "QUICK FIX" IS WHEN WE APOLOGIZE AND START AGAIN RIGHT AFTER WE HAVE TREATED SOMEONE BADLY. WE DON'T ALWAYS GET IT RIGHT, BUT WHEN WE DON'T - WE HAVE THE OPPORTUNITY TO MAKE IT RIGHT!

"Quick Fix" (or rupture and repair) acknowledges that all of us get it wrong sometimes. As caregivers, modeling a "quick fix" means that when we get it wrong (perhaps we flip our lids, perhaps we apply correction and discipline when the need was regulation and connection) we can simply acknowledge our mistake to our child. When we acknowledge that we got it wrong, not only are we repairing the connection with our kids, we're also teaching them how to use the "quick fix" tool. By some miracle of grace, repairing connection when we've gotten it wrong can actually create a stronger connection than if we had never gotten it wrong in the first place!

R REDO

A REDO IS LIKE A TIME MACHINE! WHEN WE'VE DONE SOMETHING WE KNOW WE SHOULDN'T HAVE, OR WHEN WE HAVE SAID SOMETHING WE REGRET, ASKING FOR A REDO GIVES US THE CHANCE TO START OVER AND TRY AGAIN. DID WE SHOUT WHEN WE SHOULD HAVE SAID PLEASE? ASKING FOR A REDO ALLOWS US TO TRY AGAIN THE RIGHT WAY. EVERYBODY NEEDS A SECOND CHANCE SOMETIMES!

The "redo" is usually best when we need to try a whole "scene" again. Before we move to discipline and correction mode, we can offer our kids a chance to try again the right way. This can help us avoid power struggles with our kids and model grace and kindness. Plus, if the redo works, we get the result we had originally wanted anyway, and everyone wins!

S SNACKS

EVERYBODY LOVES SNACKS, WHAT ARE SOME OF YOUR FAVORITES? HEALTHY SNACKS WITH PLENTY OF PROTEIN CAN HELP US STAY "IN THE GREEN."

Keeping our kids well hydrated and allowing plenty of access to protein snacks (like cheese sticks, nuts, beef jerky, or peanut butter) can help our kids stay regulated and "in the green." A "Yes Basket" is a popular tool among caregivers of kids who have experienced trauma. This is a basket of snacks that you will always say "yes" to when a kid asks. "Yes Baskets" build connection by meeting a kids' need over, and over. Anytime you leave the house, it's good to think about a little bag of snacks and water. Being proactive with hydration and protein can help us avoid a lot of unnecessary conflict!

T TRAUMA

TRAUMA HAPPENS WHEN WE LIVE THROUGH SOMETHING REALLY SCARY. THE WORD "TRAUMA" DESCRIBES THE EFFECT THAT THIS SCARY EXPERIENCE CAN HAVE ON US. EVERYONE HAS EXPERIENCED SOME SORT OF TRAUMA. EVERY PERSON (BIG OR LITTLE) IS PRECIOUS, AND VALUABLE, AND WORTHY OF LOVE NO MATTER WHAT!

Early childhood trauma effects our brains, bodies, biologies, behaviors, and beliefs. However, the effects of early childhood trauma can be adjusted to, or reversed. Some trauma is obvious - neglect, abuse, abandonment. Some is more subtle - early life hospitalizations, witnessing violence or a natural disaster, pre-natal issues like a stressful pregnancy or substance exposure. Taking an ACEs quiz (simply google it!) is a good way to get a sense of what trauma we are dealing with. Understanding the effects of trauma helps us give empathetic, appropriate care.

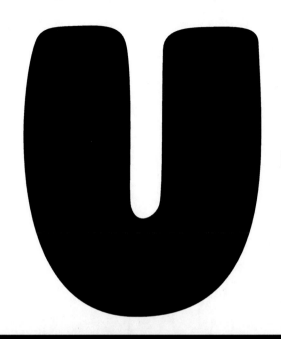

UNDERSTAND

LISTENING TO OUR FRIENDS AND OUR ADULTS IS A PATHWAY TO UNDERSTANDING THEM! UNDERSTANDING THEM HELPS US TO BE BETTER FRIENDS WITH STRONGER CONNECTIONS!

Understanding our kids has to do with knowing about how they may be affected by trauma they've experienced, but also listening with empathy, identifying needs behind behaviors (and meeting them!) and helping our kids discover their voice so they can communicate and advocate for themselves. This level of understanding is incredibly challenging, and requires daily work - but it's also beautiful, and rewarding, and healing!

U VOICE

WHAT YOU THINK AND SAY MATTERS. YOU HAVE A PLACE IN THE WORLD, AND A PART TO PLAY – YOU HAVE A VOICE!

We want to help our kids discover and use their voice. That can be a real challenge when they have a history of having needs that were not met. When a baby cries, but isn't soothed, they learn that their voice does not have an effect on the world. When our babies' needs weren't met, they began to learn that same lesson about themselves. We help our kids discover and use their voice when we are attentive to their needs, give them opportunities to make choices, or ask them what they need. When we remind our kids that they are precious, that their needs matter (and can be met) we are giving *Voice*!

W WATER

DID YOU KNOW THAT MORE THAN HALF OF YOUR BODY IS MADE OF WATER? DID YOU KNOW THAT 75% OF YOUR BRAIN IS MADE OF WATER? DID YOU KNOW THAT BY THE TIME YOU FEEL THIRSTY, YOU'RE ALREADY DEHYDRATED? OUR BODIES AND MINDS NEED WATER, SO DRINK UP!

Like protein snacks, keeping water bottles around and helping our kids stay hydrated is a simple and cheap way to help them stay "in the green" where they can think clearly. There are many simple ways to help our kids drink more water, more frequently: find water bottles they love, use simple flavorings, offer a drink before a snack, and a drink before a meal, set reminder timers, keep a cooler outside, do whatever it takes!

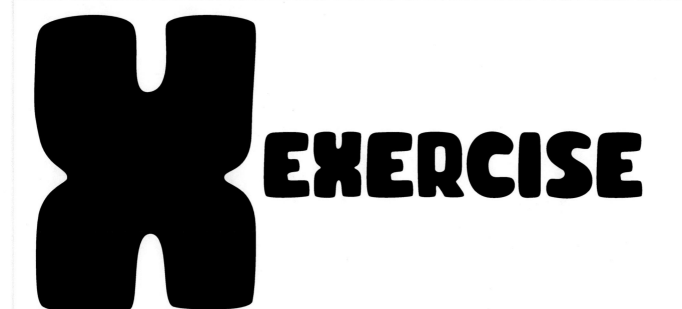

EXERCISE

EXERCISE HELPS KEEP OUR BODIES AND MINDS HEALTHY. EXERCISE CAN ALSO HELP US GET OUT EXTRA ENERGY, OR EVEN DEAL WITH BIG EMOTIONS!

WHAT ARE SOME OF YOUR FAVORITE WAYS TO EXERCISE?

Exercise is a great tool for helping kids move from "red" to "green." It can also be a great way to help meet some of our kids' sensory needs. Exercising together is a form of play that can strengthen connection. Finding ways to be active that you and your kids love can be an incredibly helpful tool in providing trauma-informed care.

YES! YES!
YES! YES
S! YES! YES! Y
ES! YES! YE
S! YES! YES! YES
YES! YE YES! YE
S! YES! S! YES!

y

YES

ARE YOU AWESOME? YES!
ARE YOU LOVED? YES, YES!
DO YOU MATTER? YES!
ARE YOU IMPORTANT? YES, YES, YES!
DO YOU HAVE NEEDS? YES!
CAN YOU DO IT? YES! YES!
YES, YES, YES, YES, YES!

Our kids have had a lot of "no" in their life, maybe you have too. Finding ways to give more "yes" answers helps us meet needs, build connection, and help our kids find their worth and voice.
Do you matter, caregiver? YES!
Is the work you do important? YES, YES!
Are you worthy of love? YES, YES, YES!!!
YES YES YES YES YES YES.

Z zzzzzzzzzzzz

THAT WAS A LOT OF READING, IT WAS SO MUCH FUN. AFTER ALL OF THAT, I'M A LITTLE BIT "IN THE BLUE," IS MY BODY TELLING ME TO TAKE A REST? YES! LET'S HAVE SOME SLEEP.

Caregiver, your work is transformative. Rest isn't easy to find when you're in the grind, but I hope that you can feel rest, and joy, and hope, and peace, and courage to carry on this great and difficult work! Thank you and goodnight!

WHAT "TRAUMA-INFORMED CARE" LOOKS LIKE

+ Recognizes the changes in brain, body, and beliefs that trauma causes in kids we care for.

+ Happens in an environment where kids feel physically and emotionally safe. Providing "felt safety" is a priority.

+ Builds on a foundation of connection. Building safe and trusting connections informs all aspects of care. Even the approach to challenging behaviors must make connection a top priority.

+ Understands and teaches regulation. Helps kids understand how to recognize when they're not regulated and gives them tools to regulate. Caregivers offer themselves as "co-regulators" which fosters "felt safety" and connection.

THE EMOTIONS THERMOMETER

The emotions thermometer is a tool that helps caregivers and kids name their feelings in real time. There are no bad emotions, understanding what we're feeling simply helps us act with more thoughtfulness and care. "What's your temperature?" or "It seems like you're feeling a little blue," are statements that can incorporate the emotions thermometer into our caregiving.

There are situations when we may want to move from one "color" to another. Having tools that help us move between colors is a vital skill in trauma-informed caregiving. You can make yourself a chart like this picture and use a clothespin as a tool to identify and name what temperature you are.

RED
MAD, HYPER, ANXIOUS, PLAYFUL, "FLIPPED LID"

GREEN
IDEAL FOR LEARNING & BUILDING RELATIONSHIPS

BLUE
SAD, CALM, TIRED, LOW ENERGY, BORED, SHY, CONTEMPLATIVE

RED TO GREEN:
DEEP BREATHING, BIG MUSCLE MOVEMENT, GOING FOR A WALK BLOWING BUBBLES

BLUE TO GREEN:
EXERCISE, PROTEIN SNACK, WATER, MUSIC

PUTTING THE LID BACK ON!

Flipping Our Lid (See "B", "F", and "L") happens when our "downstairs brain" senses danger and takes control of our brain and body. People who have experienced early life trauma tend to have powerful and overly active "downstairs brains;" they spot and sense danger more readily, and go into fight/flight/freeze more quickly.

When our lid is flipped, we don't have access to reason and future thinking. Lectures or threats of impending punishment will never land, when the lid is off.

When our kids are dysregulated, our job is to help them regulate. To help them move from "red" to "green." As we do the work of co-regulation, it's vital that we keep our own lids on. Nothing good will happen if both parties are operating with flipped lids! Job one is to simply help our kids get back to green.

Once everyone is in the green, then the important follow up conversations about consequences, expectations, or morality, can start.

Tools like: deep breathing, exercise, water (especially through a straw), and validating the emotional reality our kids are experiencing can help put the lid back on.

These ideas come from the work of Daniel Siegel M.D.

SENSORY DIET

Kids who have experienced trauma often have a chaotic or imbalanced set of sensory needs.

Some of our kids are easily overwhelmed by sensory inputs. A strong smell, loud sound, or unwelcome taste or texture can get our kids dysregulated.

Some of our kids need more inputs than we are used to, THEY'RE STARVING for sensory input! They bang toys to make noise, they agitate their friends to keep the "volume" up, they bump and bang walls everywhere they go, they fidget and squirm in their seats.

Understanding how our kids are experiencing the world through their senses can help us identify some causes of confusing and challenging behaviors.

We can find healthy ways to help our kids handle their need for sensory input. Some practical tools we can use are weighted items, sound canceling headphones, bubble gum, calming music, fidgets, physical activity, "differential seating," kinetic sand, and more!

"What is the need behind the behavior?" is one of our primary lenses for Trauma-Informed Care. Sensory needs are a common answer to this question.

GO DEEPER WITH TRAUMA-INFORMED CARE!

Search out and enjoy resources like:

The Karyn Purvis Institute of Child Development
at Texas Christian University
The Connected Parent
by Karyn Purvis, Ph.D., & Lisa Qualls with Emmelie Pickett
The Connected Child
by Karyn B. Purvis, Ph.D., David R. Cross, Ph.D., & Wendy Lyons Sunshine
The Whole-Brain Child
by Daniel J. Siegel, M.D. & Tina Payne Bryson, Ph.D.
No Drama Discipline
by Daniel J. Siegel, M.D. & Tina Payne Bryson, Ph.D.
Brainstorm
by Daniel J. Siegel, M.D.
The Body Keeps The Score
by Bessel van der Kolk, M.D.
I Love You Rituals
by Becky A. Bailey, Ph.D.
The Connected Therapist
by Marti Smith, OTR/L

Show Hope's "Hope For The Journey" annual conference
The Karyn Purvis Institute of Child Development - on YouTube
The TBRI® podcast
Find a TBRI® Practitioner in your area

THE WORK OF
THE PEARL PROJECT

The Pearl Project is a nonprofit based in Florida
that exists to offer trauma-informed education
and support to caregivers, professionals,
and the community at large.

The Pearl Project offers coaching, group trainings,
support groups, camps, retreats, and material support
to caregivers to empower them as they help kids
discover that they are precious.

Thepearlproject.org

the
pearl
project

Made in the USA
Coppell, TX
19 January 2024

27771331R10038